Spotlight On
the Internet

Jennifer Gipp

THOMSON

COURSE TECHNOLOGY

Australia • Canada • Mexico • Singapore • Spain • United Kingdom • United States

THOMSON

COURSE TECHNOLOGY

Spotlight on the Internet
by Jennifer Gipp

Executive Director, Learning Solutions:
Nicole Jones Pinard

Senior Acquisitions Editor:
Marjorie Hunt

Product Manager:
Pam Conrad

Development Editor:
Fran Marino

Editorial Assistant:
Rebecca Padrick

Senior Marketing Manager:
Joy Stark

Marketing Coordinator:
Julie Schuster

Production Editor:
Summer Hughes

Senior Manufacturing Coordinator:
Julio Esperas

Manuscript Quality Assurance Lead:
Jeffrey Schwartz

Interior Design:
BIG BLUE DOT

Art Director:
Beth Paquin

Cover Image:
Christopher Corr

Copy Editor:
Harry Johnson

Proofreader:
John Bosco

Indexer:
Joan Green

Compositor:
GEX Publishing Services

Table of Contents

Table of Contents

Preface

Computer technology is on the move! The advances can be seen and felt across society on a daily basis. As computer technology progresses, it is beginning to carve its path into the middle and elementary school levels. Though this is a scholastic discipline that is still very much in its infancy, it continues to advance and mold its importance in society.

Though many textbooks are dedicated to learners in high school or elementary school, it appears that our valued middle school learners have been left out in the dark without a dedicated text. With this in mind, Thomson Course Technology is proud to present the *Spotlight On...* middle school product line.

With the commitment to our middle school learners, we sought the authorship of an expert in grades 6-8. Jennifer Gipp is a computer technology middle school teacher at D.C. Everest Middle School in Wisconsin. She has been teaching middle school technology since 2002 and her proven lesson plans in the classroom are the foundation of this product line.

We at Course Technology recognize the importance of computer technology. In fact, we are dedicated to the progression and learning of computer technology as it makes its way to all levels of scholastic learning.

OVERVIEW

The *Spotlight On...* product line introduces middle school learners to basic technology concepts and skills through a computer application suite. With middle school learners as the focal audience for this text, *Spotlight On...* has made efforts to keep page count down, but not at the sacrifice of the essentials of computer concepts and tasks. Currently, the product line boasts an additional seven titles:

> *Spotlight On Introduction to Computers*
> *Spotlight On Word Processing*
> *Spotlight On Spreadsheets*
> *Spotlight On Presentations*
> *Spotlight On Databases*
> *Spotlight On Multimedia and Publications*
> *Spotlight On Input Technologies*

Features

The *Spotlight On...* product line is the perfect text for bridging elementary learning to the high school curriculum. This product line touts a series of features designed specifically for middle school learners.

CROSS-CURRICULAR ACTIVITIES

As time brings about change, so has technology. Currently, many states and districts have issued requirements for core disciplines to have a technological integration component. Knowing this, the *Spotlight On...* product line is committed to including substantial student projects that link technology to a core discipline. *Spotlight's* "Project Practice" touts at least four projects per chapter in the following subjects:

 Mathematics

 Science

 Language Arts

 Social Studies

 Music/Art

For *Spotlight On the Internet*, there are 16 cross-curricular "Project Practices."

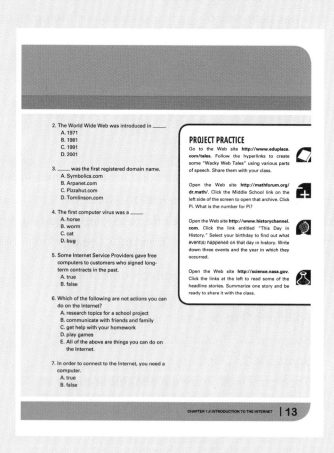

2. The World Wide Web was introduced in _____
   A. 1971
   B. 1981
   C. 1991
   D. 2001

3. _____ was the first registered domain name.
   A. Symbolics.com
   B. Arpanet.com
   C. Pizzahut.com
   D. Tomlinson.com

4. The first computer virus was a _____
   A. horse
   B. worm
   C. cat
   D. bug

5. Some Internet Service Providers gave free computers to customers who signed long-term contracts in the past.
   A. true
   B. false

6. Which of the following are not actions you can do on the Internet?
   A. research topics for a school project
   B. communicate with friends and family
   C. get help with your homework
   D. play games
   E. All of the above are things you can do on the Internet.

7. In order to connect to the Internet, you need a computer.
   A. true
   B. false

PROJECT PRACTICE

Go to the Web site **http://www.eduplace.com/tales**. Follow the hyperlinks to create some "Wacky Web Tales" using various parts of speech. Share them with your class.

Open the Web site **http://mathforum.org/dr.math/**. Click the Middle School link on the left side of the screen to open that archive. Click Pi. What is the number for Pi?

Open the Web site **http://www.historychannel.com**. Click the link entitled "This Day in History." Select your birthday to find out what event(s) happened on that day in history. Write down three events and the year in which they occurred.

Open the Web site **http://science.nasa.gov**. Click the links at the left to read some of the headline stories. Summarize one story and be ready to share it with the class.

CHAPTER 1:// INTRODUCTION TO THE INTERNET | 13

STEP-BY-STEP INSTRUCTION

Spotlight On... strives to give students valuable computer concepts that are reinforced with step-by-step instruction. This product line is unique because of its balance between creating projects from scratch and making necessary edits and changes to data files and saving the files onto a computer or disk.

PARENTAL INVOLVEMENT

Though parents are the first and foremost educators of children, at times, publishers have moved away from parental involvement. The *Spotlight On...* series recognizes the importance of parental involvement and has dedicated one project per chapter within its texts to involve a parent or guardian's input. These projects allow the student and parent or guardian to work together on a useful, relevant project that not only reinforces the concepts learned in the chapter, but also the invaluable interaction between parent and child.

WORKING TOGETHER

The *Spotlight On...* product line encourages group projects within its text. Dubbed as the "Buddy Projects" within the end of each chapter section, students are asked to work together in small groups of two or three to accomplish fun tasks that are very much related to the everyday life of a middle school learner. In each chapter, the *Spotlight On...* product line dedicates one project to the cooperation and accomplishments of group learning.

Lesson 2-3 WEB SITE INTEGRITY

IN THIS LESSON, WE WILL:
> Examine links of a Web site
> Learn guidelines that determine a good site
> Rate a Web site using an evaluation form

With so many Web sites, how do you know that what you are reading on any of them is true? Do you believe things just because you see them on the Internet? Hopefully, you don't. This lesson will help you act as a cyber sleuth to finding clues to a good, trustworthy Web site.

WEB SITE TESTING

1. Type the following address into the address box: **www.city-mankato.us** and press **Enter**; press **return** if you are using a Mac.
2. Scroll down to read the paragraph about the city of Mankato, Minnesota, and the reasons why the winter temperatures never drop below 70 degrees.
3. Click the first link to see a map of Mankato.

You will see a city map indicating all of the hot springs located throughout the city.

4. Click the **Back** arrow once.
5. Now click link **#2** to read about the history of Mankato.
6. Click the **Back** arrow again.
7. Click link **#6** to find out about the great pyramid found in Mankato.
8. Click the **Back** arrow once more.
9. Click link **#4** to find out about the Underwater City in the Mankato area.

This sounds like a great city to visit! Have you ever been to Mankato, Minnesota? Did you know these great sights were there? Or, are they?

10. Scroll all the way down to the bottom of the page.
11. Click the link entitled **Disclaimer** and read the information.

By reading the disclaimer, we discovered that some things really are too good to be true! Just because you may read something on the Internet, it does not mean that it is true. If you can't find at least one or two other sources to back up the information, chances are it is not true.

WEB SITE GUIDELINES

As a responsible Web surfer, you need to check that your site follows these guidelines before believing what you read. If not, you should keep on surfing to a more credible source!

• The information is well-organized and easy to find.
• There are clear instructions on how to use any special features of the site.
• The content is well-written with correct spelling and grammar.
• There is not too much advertising.
• The site does not promote any negative messages.
• The site does not ask you for any personal information before you can use it. If it does, close the page immediately.

26 | CHAPTER 2:// INTERNET GUIDELINES   LESSON 2-3:// WEB SITE INTEGRITY

Features

MARGINAL FEATURES

Within each chapter, students can learn valuable information from *Spotlight's* marginal features. Being colorful and donning a picturesque icon, students will be drawn to the information within its boxes. *Spotlight's* marginal features include:

 Tips and Tricks
- A means of showing students other ways of accomplishing a task

 Hint
- A reinforcement and a reminder of valuable information learned in previous lessons.

 Important Information
- Information the student must know before tackling the task.

As part of our features, we also include a very special character. Because this text is a bridge between elementary and high school learners, a support character has been added for those students that need just a little more guidance. P.D., an animated PDA (personal digital assistant), will help guide students as they explore the different computer applications.

KEY TERMS

The *Spotlight On...* product line knows the importance of good vocabulary building. Because of its importance, *Spotlight On...* includes dedicated sections for vocabulary terms on each page. Every lesson opens with a list of key terms. As the lesson continues, these key terms are bolded in the text and defined in the Important Vocabulary Terms sections in the upper and lower margins of the book.

Hi! My name is P.D.

ACKNOWLEDGEMENTS

In the creation of this book, the author would like to publicly thank the following individuals for their dedication to this new product line:

> My husband, Corey, and my children, Hunter and Olivia: thank you for your patience and understanding through the many late nights of writing and editing.

> My 6th grade Computer Skills classes at D.C. Everest Middle School for helping me to understand what works and what doesn't for the middle school learner.

> My high school business teacher, Marie C. Braatz: your dedication to students and enthusiasm for the business field are what inspired me to become a business teacher.

> Nicole Pinard, Executive Director, Learning Solutions and Marjorie Hunt, Senior Acquisitions Editor: many thanks for bringing a dedicated text to the middle school market and your confidence in me.

> Dave Rivera, Developmental Editor and Product Manager for the first four books: many thanks for being an integral part to publishing these books.

> Pam Conrad, Product Manager, and Fran Marino, Developmental Editor, for this book: thanks for your efforts with this title.

> Joy Stark, Senior Marketing Manager and Julie Schuster, Marketing Coordinator: thank you for your dedication to this product and spreading the word to our sales force. Your ingenuity for promoting these books is a valuable asset to us.

> Patty Stephan, Director of Production and Summer Hughes, Production Editor: thanks for keeping our books on schedule.

> Jeff Schwartz, Manuscript QA Project Leader: I never knew so much work went into ensuring our product was at the highest quality. Thanks so much for the testing of materials.

> Laura Rickenbach, Graphic Designer: much gratitude to guiding the team through the different design ideas and your find for a cover illustrator.

> And the entire team at Thomson Course Technology: for their hard work and dedication to quality books.

Dear Student,

Hello friend! Welcome to Spotlight on the Internet! In this book, we will learn how the Internet has grown throughout the years and how it affects our daily lives including our learning and play time. We will learn how to stay safe while on the Internet and what is safe to share with our online friends. We explore some guidelines to help you determine a trustworthy Web site. We will also use thesaurus, dictionary, encyclopedia, map, and homework help reference sites. Search engines and directories will help us find Web sites with specific information. We will also retrieve text and photos and then create citations to give credit to the authors of those sites.

I will be here throughout the textbook to help you learn about computers. I will show you examples of what your screen should look like and I will also give you hints to help you remember some of the things we have done. I am a handheld computer, which is also called a personal digital assistant or PDA. You, my friend, can call me P.D.

Computers are used in nearly every part of our lives. I'm sure you cannot even imagine what life was like before computers. Try to imagine how much harder it would have been for some companies before the invention of computers and the Internet. Can you also imagine how much harder it would have been to do a research project or find information before the Internet? You are very lucky to be learning this information now so you can use the knowledge now and in the future.

YOUR FRIEND,

P.D.

Are you ready? Let's get started!

Chapter 1
INTRODUCTION TO THE INTERNET

Think of your favorite food. Is it grandma's chocolate chip cookies, mom's chicken soup, or dad's barbequed ribs? All kinds of recipes can be found on the Internet, where you can search by recipe or even by ingredient. Traditionally, recipes would be written on note cards or torn out of magazines and then filed in a recipe box. Today, users can click Internet links to find variations on a traditional recipe or find entirely new and innovative dishes to cook.

IN THIS CHAPTER, WE WILL:
> Learn the history of the Internet
> Learn several uses of the Internet
> Learn how to connect to the Internet
> Open a browser
> Identify various parts of the Internet window
> Open a Web site
> Identify the parts of a Web site address
> Learn common domain extensions
> Use hyperlinks to visit other Web pages
> Save a Web site to a list of Favorites or Bookmarks to retrieve later

Lesson 1-1 INTERNET BASICS

IN THIS LESSON, WE WILL:
> Learn the history of the Internet
> Learn several uses of the Internet
> Learn how to connect to the Internet
> Open a browser
> Identify various parts of the Internet window

KEY TERMS
browser
home page
HTML
Internet
Internet Service Provider (ISP)
menu bar
modem
scroll bars
Standard Buttons toolbar
surfing the Web
title bar
Uniform Resource Locator (URL)
World Wide Web

Can you imagine life before the Internet? Although you probably use the Internet on a daily basis, do you really know what it is, how it started, how you connect to it, how to communicate with it, or how to use it to do research? And, how can you be sure you are doing all of these things safely? The **Internet** is a very large network that connects millions of computers around the world.

HISTORY OF THE INTERNET

The Internet has come a long way in just a few short decades. It has evolved into a very helpful resource during your lifetime. The World Wide Web was introduced in 1991, but has changed so much in a short amount of time. Here's a brief history of the major events that helped form what we know of as the Internet:

1969: ARPANET (Advanced Research Project Agency Network) connects four computers at four universities in the U.S.

1971: E-mail is invented by Ray Tomlinson.

1982: TCP/IP, the common language of all Internet computers, is developed.

1985: On March 15, Symbolics.com is given the first registered domain name.

1988: The first computer virus, a worm, attacks and shuts down 10% of all Internet hosts.

1991: The World Wide Web is released by CERN, Tim Berners-Lee developer.

1993: Mosaic, the first graphics-based Web browser, becomes available.

1994: Pizza Hut takes the first online pizza order for a mushroom and pepperoni pizza with extra cheese.

1995: AOL, Prodigy, and CompuServe offer dial-up service to the Internet for home use.

1998: Internet users judge an ice skating competition —the first time a TV sports show's outcome is determined by viewers.

IMPORTANT VOCABULARY TERMS

Internet: a very large network that connects millions of computers around the world.

1999: Internet service companies are giving free computers to customers that sign a long-term contract.

2000: Napster allows people to download free music off the Internet. A major lawsuit ends the free downloading later that year.

2003: The SQL Slammer worm takes roughly 10 minutes to spread worldwide, and disables tens of thousands of servers, impacting banks, air traffic control, and emergency (911) systems.

2005: Approximately 400 million computers are connected to the Internet.

USES OF THE INTERNET

You can use the Internet to do many things, including:

- Research topics for a school project.
- Find out more about your favorite hobby, sport, music, etc.
- Communicate with friends and family.
- Get help with your homework.
- Play games.

- Buy things (new or used).
- And lots more!

The lessons in this book will show us how to do most of the things on this list.

CONNECTING TO THE INTERNET

In order to connect to the Internet, you will need the following items:

- A modem (either internal or external)
- An Internet Service Provider (ISP)

A **modem** is the piece of equipment that lets your computer "talk" to other computers using telephone lines, cable lines, fiber optic wires, or a wireless connection. A modem can be either internal or external. The word modem comes from two words: modulator and demodulator. An **Internet Service Provider (ISP)** is the company that provides the connection service to the Internet. (Think of the ISP as the middleman between your computer and the Internet.)

---

modem: a piece of equipment that lets computers "talk" to other computers using telephone lines, cable lines, or a wireless connection. It can be internal or external.

Internet Service Provider (ISP): a company that provides the connection service to the Internet. The ISP is the middleman between your computer and the Internet.

Lesson 1-1 INTERNET BASICS

You may be surprised to know that a computer is not even necessary to connect to the Internet. You could connect to the Internet using a special keyboard and your television, a cell phone, or even a personal digital assistant (PDA).

OPENING YOUR BROWSER

Now that we know what we need to connect to the Internet, let's get started. To search the World Wide Web, we need software called a **browser**. Two common browsers are Microsoft Internet Explorer and Netscape Navigator, both of which are used on a PC. When using a MacIntosh, the most common browser is Safari. Searching the World Wide Web is also called "**surfing the Web**."

The **World Wide Web** is a system of Internet servers that support **HTML** documents. HTML stands for HyperText Markup Language, and allows users to follow links to other pages, documents, or graphics.

Sometimes schools choose to use other browsers, such as Mozilla Firefox, that offer more security against unwanted pop-ups and better filtering against inappropriate subjects.

1. Log in to your computer if you haven't already.
2. Find your browser icon on your desktop. If you are using a Mac, the browser icon can be found on the dock or in the OS folder under Applications. Your teacher will tell you the name of the browser you will be using.
3. Double-click the icon to open the program.

TIPS & TRICKS
If you do not have a shortcut to a browser on your desktop, you may need to click the Start button in the lower-left corner and find the name of the browser from there.

When you open your browser, a screen appears that is called a **home page**. Your home page is the Web page that appears when your browser is opened.

title bar: the blue bar that runs across the top of the screen that tells the name of the Web site as well as the name of the browser.

menu bar: the row of words across the top of the screen that "pull down" to reveal other commands.

Below is a picture of a home page opened with Internet Explorer.

Figure 1-01　Home page

PARTS OF THE WINDOW

Let's take a look at some of the other major parts of the Internet Explorer window. Some of the parts are very similar to those found in other Windows programs. Remember, if you are using a Mac, the parts of the window will be different.

The blue bar that runs across the top of the screen that tells the name of the Web page as well as the name of the browser is called the **title bar**. This bar also contains the Minimize, Maximize/Restore Down, and Close buttons, which are found on the far right side of the screen.

Figure 1-02　The title bar

IMPORTANT INFORMATION

All screen shots are from Microsoft Internet Explorer 6.0. If you are using a Mac, a different version of this program, or a different browser your screen will look different.

Below the blue title bar is the **menu bar**, which contains a row of words. When you click each word, a list of menu commands will appear. All commands can be executed using the menu commands. This is also called the pull down menu bar since the command choices "pull down" from the menu bar.

File　Edit　View　Favorites　Tools　Help

Figure 1-03　The menu bar

Lesson 1-1 INTERNET BASICS

IMPORTANT VOCABULARY TERMS

Standard Buttons toolbar: contains shortcuts for many common tools such as back, forward, refresh, stop, and home.

Uniform Resource Locator (URL): the address of a Web site.

You will also find a toolbar across the top of the screen. This toolbar is called the **Standard Buttons toolbar**, and it contains shortcuts for many common functions. The first two buttons on the toolbar are directional: Back and Forward, and they will take you back to the last Web page you viewed, or forward to a more current one, respectively. The Stop button is next. Clicking it stops a Web site from loading. The Refresh button is used to update any changes to a Web page such as temperature or stock prices. The Home button takes you back to your home page.

The next set of buttons opens a task pane along the left side of the screen. The Search button allows you to search the Internet for a specific topic. The Favorites button displays all Web sites you have saved. You can also add and organize your favorite Web pages from this task pane. The History button shows you all Web pages you have viewed within the past two weeks, one week, or day. Each of these three buttons acts like a toggle switch, in that they turn on with a click and turn off with another click.

When you move your mouse pointer over the buttons on the toolbar, a small pop-up label called a ScreenTip appears indicating the name of that button. We will use many of the tools on the toolbar throughout this book. If you do not see the toolbar, click View from the menu bar, and then select Toolbars. A list of all available toolbars appears. Click the one(s) that you need.

IMPORTANT INFORMATION

To find out the name of button on the toolbar, move your mouse pointer over the button. A ScreenTip appears telling you the name of that button.

Below the Standard Buttons toolbar is the Address Bar. This is where you type in the address of the Web site you would like to visit. The Web site address is also known as the **Uniform Resource Locator (URL)**.

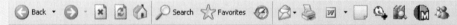

Figure 1-04   The Standard Buttons toolbar

scroll bars: the sliding bars found along the right and bottom of the screen, which allow you to see other parts of a long or wide Web page.

There are two rules to remember when typing the address or URL of a Web site:

- The entire address must be spelled correctly—including letters, numbers, and any punctuation symbols. Many times a single misspelling will take you to an entirely different Web site or give you an error message.
- Web sites do not contain any spaces. A space in a Web site address will also give you an error message.

When you finish typing the Web site address, you can either press Enter on your keyboard or you can click the green "Go" arrow on the Address Bar. If you are using a Mac, press **return**.

There are sometimes two **scroll bars** on the screen as well. One is located along the right side of the screen, and one is located along the bottom of the screen. When you have a long Web page, you can drag the button on the scroll bar up and down to see other parts. You can use the horizontal scroll bar to see parts of a wide Web page.

NOW YOU TRY IT!

Open your Internet browser. What is the home page at your school? Why do you think that Web page was chosen for the home page? What is the home page on your home computer? Why was that one chosen?

TIPS & TRICKS

Another way to display any missing toolbars is to right-click in the gray area at the top of the screen. You will see a list of all available toolbars. Click the one(s) that you need.

Lesson 1-2 EXPLORING A WEB SITE

IN THIS LESSON, WE WILL:

> Open a Web site
> Identify the parts of a Web site address
> Learn common domain extensions
> Use hyperlinks to visit other Web pages

> Save a Web site to a list of Favorites or Bookmarks to retrieve later

KEY TERMS
domain extension
Favorites
hyperlink

In this lesson, you will learn more about Web sites and how to use them to find more information or surf. If it is okay with your teacher, you may want to bring headphones to class so you can hear the sounds on the Web sites we will be visiting throughout the chapters in this book.

OPENING A WEB SITE

1. Open your browser.
2. Type the following into the Address box: **www.pbskids.org** and press **Enter** or click the Go button. If you are using a Mac, press **return**.

The following Web site appears:

Figure 1-05   The PBS Kids Web site

IMPORTANT INFORMATION
Since the Internet is constantly changing, please be aware that there may be some links in this book that have changed.

If you do not see the PBS Kids Web site, double-check the spelling of the URL that you entered. Remember, you must spell the address correctly with no spaces.

Before we start exploring this Web site, let's look at the address we just typed in:

http://www.pbskids.org

When searching the World Wide Web, the URL starts with **http://**. It is not necessary to type this section of the URL since your browser will automatically add it.

IMPORTANT VOCABULARY TERMS

domain extension: the last part of the URL indicating the type of Web site.

Let's examine the rest of the URL.

www: when a Web site starts with www., we know it is found on the World Wide Web. However, not all Web sites start with www., and many will work without it.

pbskids: the next part of the Web site gives the company or Web site name. This is sometimes very long with punctuation marks such as (.), (_), or (/) found inside of it.

org: the last part of the URL is called the **domain extension**, and tells us the type of Web site we are viewing.

COMMON DOMAIN EXTENSIONS

The extension of a URL will usually tell the type of Web site. Domain extensions indicate nonprofit organizations, governmental agencies, and businesses among many others.

Nonprofit organizations have URLs that end in **.org** (e.g., www.seaworld.org or www.girlscouts.org).

Most businesses have URLs that end in **.com** (e.g., www.nike.com or www.oldnavy.com).

Governmental agencies have URLs that end in **.gov** (e.g., www.fbi.gov or www.whitehouse.gov).

Military branches have URLs that end in **.mil** (e.g., www.navy.mil or www.army.mil).

Many schools, colleges, and universities have URLs that end in **.edu** (e.g., www.uwec.edu or www.stanford.edu).

E-mail providers have URLs that end in **.net** (e.g., www.earthlink.net or www.charter.net).

Public school districts often have URLs that end in **.k12**, the **two-letter state abbreviation**, and then the letters **.us** (e.g., www.dce.k12.wi.us or www.stillwater.k12.mn.us).

If you get a chance, explore the different sites and domains listed here.

Lesson 1-2 EXPLORING A WEB SITE

IMPORTANT VOCABULARY TERMS

hyperlink: a picture, object, or different colored text that will take you to another part of a Web site, a different Web site, or a file for more information.

Favorites: Web sites that are saved into a special folder on the computer for easy retrieval. When using a Mac, these are called Bookmarks.

HYPERLINKS

We will use the PBS Kids Web site to explore several **hyperlinks**, which will take us to other parts of the Web site or to a different Web site entirely. You may even be routed to a file, document, or photo. When your mouse pointer is placed over the link, it will change from an arrow to a little white hand.

1. Move your mouse pointer over the list at the left-hand side of the screen. The text changes and the characters in the circle change to reflect the one you are pointing to.
2. Click the **Cyberchase** link in the list.

The Cyberchase site opens up.

Figure 1-06   The Cyberchase Web site

3. This site usually has a weekly vote that students can participate in. If available, click the **Weekly Vote** link.
4. Answer the question, select your age, if necessary, and click **Vote** to see how your answer stacks up against other kids across the country.
5. Click the **Back** button twice to return to the main Cyberchase Web site.
6. The next thing we are going to do is play a game. Click the **Games Central** link on the right.

There are several games that relate to the Cyberchase television show.

7. Find the game entitled **Bugs in the System**. Click the link to open the game.
8. Click **Play** to start playing.

This game will test your ability to use the mouse quickly. Click a bug and drag it to the corresponding color of the bar graph on the right. It's harder than it sounds; good luck!

9. Once you have cleaned up all six rooms, play another game or two.
10. Click the **Back** arrow twice to return to the main Cyberchase Web site.

This is a pretty cool Web site; let's add it to our Favorites or Bookmarks so we can retrieve it later. Web sites that you visit can be saved into a special folder on your computer called your **Favorites** or **Bookmarks**. The great thing about saving your Web sites this way is that you don't have to remember the Web site address.

11. Click the word **Favorites** at the top of the screen. Choose **Add to Favorites** and click **OK**.

Now if you ever want to play those games again, you will just need to open your browser, click Favorites or Bookmarks, and then find the site in the list.

NOW YOU TRY IT!

Open the Web site *www.quizhub.com*. Add it to your Favorites or Bookmarks. This site has several learning and thinking games to play. Follow the links and have fun.

Chapter 1
WRAP UP

> The first computers were connected in 1969.

> The first computer virus attacked computers in 1988.

> People can research, communicate, get assistance, play games, and buy things on the Internet.

> A modem and an Internet Service Provider are necessary to connect to the Internet.

> Modems can be internal or external.

> Two common Internet browsers for a PC are Microsoft Internet Explorer and Netscape Navigator.

> The home page is the Web page that appears when the browser opens.

> A Web site address is also called a Uniform Resource Locator (URL).

> The URL of a Web site must be spelled correctly with no spaces in order for it to work correctly.

> It is not necessary to type http:// at the beginning of a Web site address.

> Domain extensions identify the type of Web site.

> Some common domain extensions are .com, .org, .mil, .net, .gov, and .edu.

> Clicking a hyperlink will take you to another part of a Web site or a different Web site or other file.

> A mouse pointer placed over a hyperlink changes from an arrow to a little white hand.

> Commonly visited Web sites can be saved to the Favorites or Bookmarks folder for easy retrieval later.

WHAT DO YOU KNOW?

1. The _____ is a very large network connecting millions of computers around the world.
   A. World Wide Web
   B. Internet
   C. Network
   D. Web site

2. The World Wide Web was introduced in _____.
   A. 1971
   B. 1981
   C. 1991
   D. 2001

3. _____ was the first registered domain name.
   A. Symbolics.com
   B. Arpanet.com
   C. Pizzahut.com
   D. Tomlinson.com

4. The first computer virus was a _____.
   A. horse
   B. worm
   C. cat
   D. bug

5. Some Internet Service Providers gave free computers to customers who signed long-term contracts in the past.
   A. true
   B. false

6. Which of the following are not actions you can do on the Internet?
   A. research topics for a school project
   B. communicate with friends and family
   C. get help with your homework
   D. play games
   E. All of the above are things you can do on the Internet.

7. In order to connect to the Internet, you need a computer.
   A. true
   B. false

PROJECT PRACTICE

Go to the Web site **www.eduplace.com/tales**. Follow the hyperlinks to create some "Wacky Web Tales" using various parts of speech. Share them with your class.

Open the Web site **http://mathforum.org/dr.math/**. Click the Middle School link on the left side of the screen to open that archive. Click Pi. What is the number for Pi?

Open the Web site **www.historychannel.com**. Click the link entitled "This Day in History." Select your birthday to find out what event(s) happened on that day in history. Write down three events and the year in which they occurred.

Open the Web site **http://science.nasa.gov**. Click the links at the left to read some of the headline stories. Summarize one story and be ready to share it with the class.

Chapter 1
WRAP UP

8. A _____ is the piece of equipment that lets your computer "talk" to other computers using telephone lines, cable lines, or a wireless connection.
   A. modem
   B. computer
   C. provider
   D. connection

9. ISP stands for _____.
   A. Internet Special Protection
   B. Internet Service Person
   C. Important Seasonal Provider
   D. Internet Service Provider

10. The software needed to easily surf the World Wide Web is called a(n) _____.
    A. Internet
    B. browser
    C. HTML document
    D. surfer

11. Your home page is the Web page that appears when your browser is opened.
    A. true
    B. false

12. The _____ button on the Standard Buttons toolbar stops a Web site from loading.
    A. Forward
    B. Refresh
    C. Stop
    D. Home

13. The Web site address is also called the Unicorn Resource Locator.
    A. true
    B. false

14. A URL cannot contain spaces.
    A. true
    B. false

15. Non-profit organizations have URLs that end in _____.
    A. .org
    B. .com
    C. .gov
    D. .mil

16. Most businesses have URLs that end in _____.
    A. .pub
    B. .bus
    C. .com
    D. .ppl

BUDDY PROJECT

Open the Web site **http://www.countryreports.org**. Work with a partner to find the following basic information about a country. Be prepared to share your findings with the class.

- capital city
- government type
- population
- languages
- life expectancy
- currency
- top two exports
- highest point

GUIDED PRACTICE

Ask your parent or guardian if his or her workplace has a Web site. Open the Web site and explore the hyperlinks. Share your findings with the class.

Chapter 2
INTERNET GUIDELINES

When businesses need to hire a new employee, they have a greater amount of information available to them than they did 20 years ago. Human Resource directors can use the Internet to request background checks on potential employees to find out if they have a criminal record. They can even run a credit check on them. After employees are hired, the employer can monitor the employees' Internet and e-mail usage. Likewise, the administration can monitor students' Internet and e-mail usage when they use school computers.

IN THIS CHAPTER, WE WILL:

> Learn what information is safe to share when online
> Review rules for polite online communication
> Answer questions relating to online safety
> Determine the best choices for safety
> Print a Web license
> Identify major common features of an e-mail program

> Differentiate between Cc and Bcc
> Learn how to add humor and personality to messages
> Send an e-mail
> Send an electronic greeting card
> Learn the difference between blogging and chatting
> Examine links of a Web site
> Learn guidelines that determine a good site
> Rate a Web site using an evaluation form

Lesson 2-1 ONLINE SAFETY

IN THIS LESSON, WE WILL:
> Learn what information is safe to share when online
> Review rules for polite online communication
> Answer questions relating to online safety
> Determine the best choices for safety
> Print a Web license

KEY TERMS
flaming
netiquette

In this lesson, you will learn more about things that you should or should not share when you are online. You will also learn the rules you need to follow when you are on the Internet.

ONLINE DOS AND DON'TS
The Internet has lots of fun sites and things to do. However, there are certain rules to remember to help keep you safe while surfing:

- Talk to your parents about setting up rules for going online.
- Don't send a photo of yourself or give out your name, address, or other personal information without your parents' consent.
- Don't give anyone your password.
- Don't agree to meet someone in person whom you have only met online.
- Don't open any files or attachments from anyone that you don't know.
- Remember, people are not always who they say they are. Just because someone says she is a 12-year-old girl who likes to play basketball, doesn't mean it's true.

- Only chat with people on your approved buddy list.
- Tell your parents about anything that makes you feel uncomfortable.

To help keep you safe, be sure that your parents always know who you are talking to online as well as the Web sites that you are visiting.

NETIQUETTE
Next, we will visit a Web site to learn about Internet safety and etiquette. The guidelines for polite interaction while online are called **netiquette**. The word netiquette is made up from the words Internet and etiquette.

Some netiquette rules to remember include:

- Don't type in all capital letters; that's like SHOUTING.
- Use correct spelling, punctuation, and grammar. Common abbreviations are acceptable.

IMPORTANT VOCABULARY TERMS

netiquette: guidelines for polite online interaction; the word is formed from Internet and etiquette.

flaming: sending angry e-mail messages.

- Don't forward chain letters or other hoaxes.
- Don't write anything about yourself or another person that you don't want shared with the world.
- Don't send angry messages; that is called **flaming**.
- Try to keep your messages short. Remember the acronym K.I.S.S. (Keep It Short & Simple).

Now, let's go online to learn more!

1. Open the browser and type the following URL into the Address box: **www.disney.go.com/ surfswell** and press **Enter**; press **return** if you are using a Mac.
2. Once the site has loaded, click **START** to begin. Then, click **GO TO ISLAND**.
3. Click "**PRIVACY FALLS**." You will need to answer a series of questions regarding what is okay to share with your online pals.
4. Continue along the path, answering the questions found in the "VIRUS CAVE," the "TEMPLE OF TACT," and the "CHALLENGE OF DOOM."

Watch the message at the bottom of the screen. As you finish the questions of a section, another word appears in the secret message.

5. Once you finish all sections, go to the "**TREASURE PALACE**" and click "**COMIC CREATOR**." Select a character and click **Next**.
6. In the story title, enter your class hour/day.
7. In the name box, enter your first name and initial of your last name.
8. In the big text box at the bottom, enter the four-word phrase that appeared when you finished all of the questions. Click **Next**.
9. Click **Print** to print your comic creation and hand it in to your teacher.

Remember your "netiquette." Always treat yourself and others with respect when corresponding online. Never write anything that you don't want others to read.

MORE ONLINE SAFETY AND NETIQUETTE SITES

Let's visit another Web site that reinforces the rules we learned earlier in the lesson.

1. Type the following URL into the Address box: **www.kids.gov** and press **Enter**; press **return** if you are using a Mac.

The following screen appears:

FirstGov for Kids

Search

Federal Citizen Information Center Home

Welcome to the U.S. government interagency Kids' Portal. This site was developed and is maintained by the Federal Citizen Information Center. It provides links to Federal kids' sites along with some of the best kids' sites from other organizations all grouped by subject. Explore, learn, have fun and don't forget to add us to your favorites!

Web Treasure Hunt
(.pdf version)

| Arts | Careers | Computers | Fighting Crime |
| Fun Stuff | Geography | Global Village | Government |

Figure 2-01   The FirstGov for Kids Web site

2. Click the "**Computers**" link.
3. Click the link entitled "**Are you a Safe Cyber Surfer?**" to find out if you know how to be safe while online.

4. Click the **Back** arrow to return to the Computers section of the FirstGov site.
5. Click the "**Cyberethics for Kids**" link. Are you a good "cybercitizen"?
6. Click the **Back** arrow again.
7. Scroll down a little further and click the "**Internet Super Heroes**" link. Click the characters on the right to find out how to deal with cyberbullies.
8. Explore some of the other links. Add this site to your favorites.

Did you see any examples of the online rules and netiquette guidelines we discussed earlier?

WEB LICENSE

Let's see just how much you have learned about being safe while on the Internet. When you answer all questions correctly, you will receive your own "Official Web License" indicating that you are a safe surfer.

1. Open your browser if necessary.
2. Type the following into the Address box: **www.pbskids.org/bts/license** and press **Enter**; press **return** if you are using a Mac.

The following site opens:

Figure 2-02 The PBS Kids Web License site

3. Type your first name in the box. Remember, your first name is not specific to only you, so it is usually a safe thing to give out on the Internet.

4. Click **drive**.

5. Click each of the links around the "road," answering the questions as you go. As you answer each question correctly, that part of the map is colored in.

6. When you are finished, choose the **Boys** or **Girls** link and print out your "license." Next, check the boxes, sign the license, and hand it in to your teacher for grading.

NOW YOU TRY IT!

Open the Web site **www.wiredkids.org/wiredkids_ org.html**. Click on the Tweens link. Read more about online safety specific to students your age. Click the link on the left side to play the BONUS.COM online safety game.

Lesson 2-2 ONLINE COMMUNICATION

IN THIS LESSON, WE WILL:

> Identify the major common features of an e-mail program
> Differentiate between Cc and Bcc
> Learn how to add humor and personality to messages

> Send an e-mail
> Send an electronic greeting card
> Learn the difference between blogging and chatting

KEY TERMS

Address Book
Attach button
Bcc: text box
blog
Cc: text box

The Internet has been a great tool for communicating with people not only across town, but across the country, and all over the world.

ELECTRONIC MAIL

The first type of communication we will cover is **e-mail**. E-mail is short for electronic mail. A very popular e-mail program is Outlook Express by Microsoft. Outlook Express is used on a PC. If you are using a Mac, your e-mail program will be different. Sometimes schools use an e-mail program called GroupWise.

Regardless of the program, most programs use similar features to compose a message.

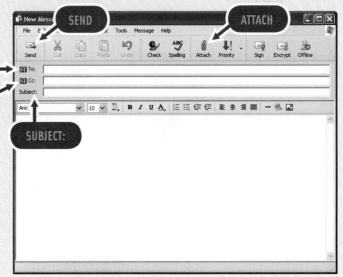

Figure 2-03   The New Message dialog box

The **"To:" text box** is where you type the e-mail address of the person you want to send the message to. Remember, you must type the e-mail address correctly. If you have saved names in your Address Book, it may be possible just to type the name of the person to whom you want to send the e-mail rather than typing the whole e-mail address. This depends on how you saved the name and address in your Address Book. The **Address Book** in your computer is very similar to a paper address book in that it holds people's names and addresses.

IMPORTANT VOCABULARY TERMS

e-mail: electronic mail.

To: text box: where you type the e-mail address of the person you want to send a message to.

Address Book: file on your computer that holds names and e-mail addresses.

chat room
cyberbullying
E-cards
e-mail
emoticons
Send button

Subject: text box
To: text box

The **"Cc:" text box** is where you can indicate another person's e-mail address so they will receive a copy of the message. Cc stands for Carbon Copy and dates back to the time when people had to use a sheet of carbon paper between pages to make a copy when typing on a typewriter. The receiver knows the person in the Cc: text box received a copy. Sometimes you will also see a **"Bcc:" text box**. Bcc stands for Blind Carbon Copy. If you place an e-mail address in the Bcc box, the receiver does not know that this person received a copy of the message.

The **Subject: text box** is an important feature for the receiver because it will tell what the message is about. Many times, people determine when or if they will read an e-mail message based on the subject. The receiver is able to see the subject line before they open the message. It is a good idea to delete an e-mail message if you do not know the sender or are uncomfortable with the subject of the message.

When you want to send a file or document along with the e-mail, you click the **Attach button**. Usually, the Attach button is indicated by a paper clip graphic.

The New Message dialog box shown in the figure also has a formatting toolbar enabling you to change the font, size, and style of the message. Be careful about using formatting since some e-mail accounts do not recognize the text formatting, and will display codes in your message. When you are finished writing the message and entering the addresses, you should click the **Send button** to send the message.

The great thing about e-mail is that you can communicate with people very quickly. When you use e-mail, remember the netiquette rules that we learned in the last lesson.

Cc: text box: an e-mail address is typed in this box to send a copy of the message; the receiver knows it has been sent to the other person.

Bcc: text box: an e-mail address is typed in this box to send a copy of a message; however, the receiver does not know it has been sent to someone else.

Subject: textbox: tells what the message is about. The receiver can see the subject of the message before opening it.

Attach button: click this to send a file or document along with your e-mail message.

Send button: click this to send the message.

Lesson 2-2 ONLINE COMMUNICATION

IMPORTANT VOCABULARY TERMS

emoticons: also known as smileys; expressions you create from the characters on your keyboard to add humor and personality to the message.

E-card: greeting card that is opened in a person's e-mail box.

To add humor and personality to your messages, use **emoticons**, also known as smileys, which are expressions you create from the characters on your keyboard. A few popular ones include:

:-)	Happy	:-e	Disappointed
:-(	Sad	:-<	Mad
:-O	Surprised	:-D	Laughing
:-@	Screaming	;-)	Winking

If you have e-mail access, you can use it to send your teacher an e-mail message. Ask your teacher for his/her e-mail address.

E-CARDS

You can also use the Internet to send cyber greetings or E-cards. An **E-card** is a greeting card that is sent to and opened in a person's e-mail box.

1. Type the following into the Address box: **www. hallmark.com** and press **Enter**; press **return** if you are using a Mac.

The Hallmark screen appears. Depending on the time of year, the layout and design of this site will vary.

2. Look for "OUR PRODUCTS" at the bottom of the page, then click **Free E-Cards**.

Figure 2-04   Free E-Cards on the Hallmark.com site

You will see all cards divided into categories at the left side of the screen.

3. Click the "**Just Because**" category.
4. Click a sub-category and then click a card. Once you choose the card you want to send, click **Personalize**.
5. Log into the site, or create an account and then log in.
6. Where it asks for the receiver's e-mail address, type your teacher's e-mail address (be sure you spell it correctly without spaces).
7. In the text box that says "your name," type in your first name and the first letter of your last name.
8. Type your e-mail address.
9. Make sure to select today's date to send the card.
10. Click **Preview E-Card**.
11. If everything looks okay, click **Send**.

blog: online personal journal; short for Web log.

chat room: virtual room where many people can communicate with each other.

cyberbullying: sending rude e-mails, gossiping, or spreading rumors about another person online.

BLOGS AND CHAT ROOMS

Although most schools block blog sites and chat rooms, it is important for you to know a little about them since you may use them outside of school.

A **blog** is an online personal journal. Blog is short for Web log. Be careful what you post to a blog since it can also be read by anyone on the Internet. Remember the online rules you learned earlier in this chapter about not sharing personal or identifying information.

Chat rooms are a great way to communicate with several friends at once. A **chat room** is not actually a real room, it is a virtual room. However, it is best to visit only those chat rooms that are restricted to the specific people on an approved list of your friends.

CYBERBULLYING

If you receive rude e-mails, or are the victim of gossip or rumors posted on the Internet, it is called **cyberbullying**, and there are several things you can do. If it happens at school, the first thing you should do is tell your teacher or principal. Also be sure to keep copies of e-mails or print out copies of inappropriate postings.

When it comes to cyberbullying, one of the best defenses is to ignore it. This can also include blocking the bully's screen name or e-mail address. You should also be sure to tell your parents. They can help you change your screen name, e-mail address, and password. If these things do not help, contact the Internet Service Provider (ISP), Web site, cell phone company, or the police.

Always remember to tell your parents about anything that makes you feel uncomfortable online—even if it is a message from a friend, or so-called friend.

NOW YOU TRY IT!

Visit the Hallmark Web site again. If your parents have an e-mail address, send them an E-card for a special holiday, or just to say thanks for all they have done for you.

Lesson 2-3 WEB SITE INTEGRITY

IN THIS LESSON, WE WILL:
> Examine links of a Web site
> Learn guidelines that determine a good site
> Rate a Web site using an evaluation form

With so many Web sites, how do you know that what you are reading on any of them is true? Do you believe things just because you see them on the Internet? Hopefully, you don't. This lesson will help you act as a cyber sleuth to finding clues to a good, trustworthy Web site.

WEB SITE TESTING

1. Type the following into the Address box: **www.city-mankato.us** and press **Enter**; press **return** if you are using a Mac.
2. Scroll down to read the paragraph about the city of Mankato, Minnesota, and the reasons why the winter temperatures never drop below 70 degrees.
3. Click the first link to see a map of Mankato.

You will see a city map indicating all of the hot springs located throughout the city.

4. Click the **Back** arrow once.
5. Now click link **#2** to read about the history of Mankato.
6. Click the **Back** arrow again.
7. Click link **#6** to find out about the great pyramid found in Mankato.
8. Click the **Back** arrow once more.
9. Click link **#4** to find out about the Underwater City in the Mankato area.

This sounds like a great city to visit! Have you ever been to Mankato, Minnesota? Did you know these great sights were there? Or, are they?

10. Scroll all the way down to the bottom of the page.
11. Click the link entitled **Disclaimer** and read the information.

By reading the disclaimer, we discovered that some things really are too good to be true! Just because you may read something on the Internet, it does not mean that it is true. If you can't find at least one or two other sources to back up the information, chances are it is not true.

WEB SITE GUIDELINES

As a responsible Web surfer, you need to check that your site follows these guidelines before believing what you read. If not, you should keep on surfing to a more credible source!

- The information is well-organized and easy to find.
- There are clear instructions on how to use any special features of the site.
- The content is well-written with correct spelling and grammar.
- There is not too much advertising.
- The site does not promote any negative messages.
- The site does not ask you for any personal information before you can use it. If it does, close the page immediately.

IMPORTANT INFORMATION

Remember, anyone with a computer and some knowledge about the Internet can create a Web page. That's why it is always a good idea to double-check the information you find on the Internet. If you can't find another site to back up the information, chances are it is not true!

NOW YOU TRY IT!

Use the Web page evaluation form to evaluate the following Web site: **www.nationalgeographic. com/pyramids**. How does it score? Would this be a good site to use for research?

1. Open the Web page evaluation form from the data disk.
2. Use the evaluation form to rate the Mankato site. How does it score?

Chapter 2
WRAP UP

> Make sure you talk to your parents about setting up rules for going online.
> Don't give out your name, address, or other personal information without your parents' consent.
> Don't give anyone your password.
> Don't agree to meet someone in person whom you have only met online.
> Don't send a photo or anything else to anyone without checking with your parents first.
> Don't open any files or attachments from anyone that you don't know.
> Remember, people are not always who they say they are.
> Only chat with people on your approved buddy list.
> Tell your parents about anything that makes you feel uncomfortable.
> Don't type in all capital letters; that's like SHOUTING.
> Use correct spelling, punctuation, and grammar. Common abbreviations are acceptable.
> Don't forward chain letters or other hoaxes.
> Don't write anything about a person that you don't want shared with the world.
> Don't send angry messages; that is called flaming.
> Try to keep your messages short. Remember the acronym K.I.S.S. (Keep It Short & Simple).
> Emoticons can add humor and personality to a message.
> Check a Web site for accuracy, integrity, and timeliness before believing what you read.

WHAT DO YOU KNOW?

1. It is okay to give your home address to someone online.
   A. true
   B. false

2. When a person says they are a 13-year-old girl in a chat room, they could actually be a 65-year-old man.
   A. true
   B. false

3. Guidelines for polite online interaction are called _____.
   A. rules
   B. netiquette
   C. chatting
   D. blogging

4. Sending angry messages is called _____.
   A. chatting
   B. blogging
   C. flaming
   D. slamming

5. It is okay to share your password with your friends.
   A. true
   B. false

6. Your computer can get a virus by opening an e-mail.
   A. true
   B. false

7. Which of the following is usually a safe piece of information to share online?
   A. your first name
   B. the name of your school
   C. your street address
   D. your phone number

PROJECT PRACTICE

Your school will be celebrating "Online Safety Week." Create a poster describing the importance of Online Safety that can be hung in the hallways to remind students how to be safe while online.

Open the Web site **www.coolmath.com**. Using the Web site evaluation form on the data disk, evaluate this Web site. How does it score?

Open the Web site **www.livinginternet.com**. Click the Email link to find out when e-mail was invented and by whom.

People around the world are battling a variety of sicknesses, from cancer to diabetes to AIDS. With the vast amount of medical Web sites available, why would the patients be concerned with Web site integrity?

8. E-mail is short for _____ mail.
   A. electric
   B. elevator
   C. especially
   D. electronic

9. When you want to send a copy of an e-mail to another person without the original recipient knowing, you should type the address in the _____ text box.
   A. Bcc:
   B. To:
   C. Cc:
   D. Subject:

10. The Attach button is usually indicated by a _____.
    A. thumb tack
    B. staple
    C. paper clip
    D. rubber band

11. Smileys or _____ can be used to add humor and personality to your messages.
    A. emotionals
    B. emphysema
    C. empties
    D. emoticons

12. A _____ is an online personal journal.
    A. blog
    B. diary
    C. flog
    D. journal

13. If you are the victim of cyberbullying, you should _____.
    A. tell your teacher or principal
    B. ignore the bully
    C. contact the ISP, Web site, or police
    D. All of the above are good responses to cyberbullying.

BUDDY PROJECT

Work with a partner to send an e-mail message to your local police department asking them why Internet safety is important. Also ask them for any suggestions to help keep you safe while online. Share your responses with the class.

GUIDED PRACTICE

Sit down with your parent or guardian and establish a list of expectations they have for you when you are online. Be sure to include the amount of time you are allowed to be online everyday, whether homework has to be completed first, and which Web sites or chat rooms you can visit. Also include guidelines for where you will be allowed to go online—in an open area in the house or in your room with the door open. Place it all in writing, including the consequences you will face if the rules are broken.

Chapter 3
REFERENCE SITES

Do you play video games? If so, you have probably found several Web sites that offer "cheat codes" for specific games. These cheat codes can help by giving you hints to shortcuts that will win the game or strategies for how to gain more power or lives as you play. Just as there are specific sites for these codes, there are reference sites where you can find a dictionary, thesaurus, encyclopedia, maps, and even help with your homework.

IN THIS CHAPTER, WE WILL:

> Use an online dictionary to find the definition of words
> Find synonyms and antonyms for words
> Learn a new word through the "Daily Buzzword"
> Do research using an online encyclopedia
> Refine a search using quotation marks
> View a city road map
> View photos taken from a satellite

> View a physical map
> View a specialized map
> Use a legend to read a map
> Find directions from school to home
> Zoom in and out of a map
> View homework help sites
> Play games related to class work
> Translate words online

Lesson 3-1 USING AN ONLINE DICTIONARY, THESAURUS, OR ENCYCLOPEDIA

IN THIS LESSON, WE WILL:
> Use an online dictionary to find the definition of words
> Find synonyms and antonyms for words
> Learn a new word through the "Daily Buzzword"
> Do research using an online encyclopedia
> Refine a search using quotation marks

KEY TERMS
antonym
synonym
wiki

Have you ever had "writer's block" and not been able to think of the perfect word to finish your sentence? Or, when reading, how often do you come across a word that you don't understand or can't define? In this lesson, we will learn how to use an online dictionary, thesaurus, and encyclopedia to help solve such problems.

DICTIONARY AND THESAURUS

1. Open your browser.
2. Type the following into the Address box: **www. hyperdictionary.com** and press **Enter**; press **return** if you are using a Mac.

The following screen appears:

Figure 3-01   The Hyperdictionary Web site

IMPORTANT INFORMATION
Remember, if you are using a browser other than Internet Explorer or if you are using a Mac, your screen might look different.

3. This site will be helpful in many of your other classes. It should be added to your list of Favorites or Bookmarks.
4. Type the word **plagiarism** in the search box and click **Search**.

TIPS & TRICKS
On many Web sites, you can just press Enter (or return if you are using a Mac) after typing text in a search box.

5. Take out a piece of paper and write the word "plagiarism" and the two definitions listed.

When you are writing the definition of a word, it is okay to copy it word for word since you are not claiming that it is your own work.

synonym: a word that means the same as another word.

antonym: a word that means the opposite of another word.

In addition to finding the definitions of words, we can also use this site to find synonyms. A **synonym** is a word that means the same as another word.

6. Type the word **sad** in the search box and click **Search**.

7. Scroll down and look for the Synonyms section.

8. Write the word "sad" on your piece of paper along with two synonyms that you found on the site.

We will also use this same site to find antonyms. An **antonym** is a word that means the opposite of another word.

9. Type the word **good** in the search box and click **Search**.

10. Scroll down and look for the Antonyms section.

11. Write the word "good" on your piece of paper along with two antonyms that you found on the site.

MORE DICTIONARY SITES

1. Type the following into the Address box: **www.wordcentral.com** and press **Enter**; press **return** if you are using a Mac.

The following screen should appear:

Figure 3-02   The Word Central Web site
By permission. From Merriam-Webster's Word Central (www.WordCentral.com)
©2006 by Merriam-Webster, Incorporated (www.Merriam-Webster.com).

This is also a good site for a dictionary; however, it does not have a thesaurus.

2. Type the word **kid** in the search box and click **Find**.

3. How many entries are listed for this word? Write your answer on your sheet of paper.

This site is a little different than the last dictionary site we visited in that it offers several other activities.

4. Click the **Back** arrow to return to the main Word Central screen.

5. Click the picture in the middle of the screen to "Enter the hallway" for some other fun activities.

Lesson 3-1
USING AN ONLINE DICTIONARY, THESAURUS, OR ENCYCLOPEDIA

IMPORTANT VOCABULARY TERMS

wiki: a Web site where all content is created and edited by its viewers.

6. Click **See my Daily BUZZWORD**. If you have speakers available, click hear it and listen to the word. Are you a "word whiz"? Write the daily buzzword and its definition on your sheet of paper.

7. Add this site to your list of favorites.

ENCYCLOPEDIA

In this lesson, you will learn how to use an online encyclopedia. Some encyclopedia sites require a subscription in order for you to access the articles. Your school may have a subscription to a site such as the World Book Online Reference Center (www.worldbookonline.com).

There are also free, open content encyclopedias with all content created and edited by the Web site's viewers. This type of Web site is called a **wiki**. A very popular open content encyclopedia is www.wikipedia.org.

1. Open your browser if it is not already open.
2. Type the following into the Address box: **www.infoplease.com/encyclopedia** and press **Enter**; press **return** if you are using a Mac.

The following site opens:

Figure 3-03   The Infoplease Encyclopedia site

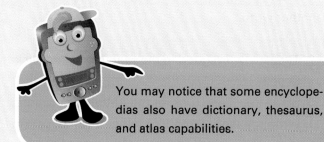

You may notice that some encyclopedias also have dictionary, thesaurus, and atlas capabilities.

This site searches the Columbia Encyclopedia, Sixth Edition.

3. Type the name **Walt Disney** in the search box and click **go!**
4. Click the first article entry entitled "Walt Disney."
5. Read the article to find out the specific year Walt Disney first created the Mickey Mouse cartoon character.

6. Take out a piece of paper and write down this information.
7. Click the **Back** arrow two times to return to the main encyclopedia page.
8. Type the words **roller coaster** in the search box and click **go!**

As we examine the results, it is clear that the search should be refined. When you search using more than one word, any article containing either word is found. However, if you place the words in quotation marks, only those articles that contain the exact string of words in that specific order will appear.

9. At the top of the screen, add quotation marks (") before the word roller and after the word coaster in the search box.

TIPS & TRICKS

There should not be any spaces before or after the quotation marks in the search box.

10. Click the **Search** button.
11. Click to open the first feature article about roller coasters.

12. Read the article, and answer the following questions on your piece of paper:
   • In what century was the roller coaster invented?
   • In which country was the roller coaster invented?
   • Where was the first American roller coaster built?
   • In what year was it built?
13. Write your name on the paper and hand it in to your teacher.

NOW YOU TRY IT!

Open the Hyperdictionary Web site and search for the definition of **hoax**. Write down the definition. Also search the Word Central Web site for the same word and write that definition down. Are the definitions similar? Was one site easier to use than the other? If so, which one?

Lesson 3-2 USING ONLINE ATLASES AND MAPS

IN THIS LESSON, WE WILL:

> View a city road map
> View photos taken from a satellite
> View a physical map
> View a specialized map

> Use a legend to read a map
> Find directions from school to home
> Zoom in and out of a map

KEY TERMS

legend
satellite map

You have probably used a map before in your Social Studies class to find a specific country or state. You may have even used a map to help your parents find the way to your vacation destination. In this lesson, you will learn how to use an online atlas and interactive map.

ATLAS

1. Open your browser.
2. Type the following into the Address box: **www. nationalgeographic.com/mapmachine** and press **Enter**; press **return** if you are using a Mac.

The following site should open:

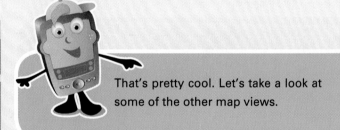

Figure 3-04   The MapMachine Web site

This site is great because it offers not only a road map, but also satellite and physical atlases, in addition to other theme maps such as average temperature or population.

3. Make sure the **ROAD MAP** tab is selected. Type **Green Bay, WI** in the search box under the ROAD MAP tab and click **FIND A PLACE**.
4. Click the **plus sign** on the left side of the screen two times to zoom in a little more.
5. Now click the **left** directional arrow two times to pan west.
6. Click the **down** arrow to pan south.
7. Scroll down the map. You should see a purple square with the words "Lambeau Field" on it. This is where the Green Bay Packers play football.

That's pretty cool. Let's take a look at some of the other map views.

8. Click the **SATELLITE** tab at the top.

satellite map: aerial photographs taken from a satellite in the Earth's atmosphere.

legend: chart that illustrates the symbols or colors on a map.

A **satellite map** is an aerial photograph taken from a satellite in the Earth's atmosphere. Do you still see Lambeau Field? The stadium is a circle within a large, grey rectangle, which is the parking lot. You can zoom in more to see it a little closer.

9. Zoom out so you can see the entire state of Wisconsin.
10. Now click the **PHYSICAL** tab to see the lay of the land.

Let's take a look at the last type of maps offered on this site.

11. Click the last tab entitled **MORE THEME MAPS**.
12. Click **Weather**, **Average Weather**, and then **Snow Cover**.
13. Click **APPLY** to see the map.

The state is mostly dark and light green. Scroll down through the **LEGEND** to see the number of days of snow cover that those colors correspond to. The **legend** is a chart that illustrates the symbols or colors on a map.

14. Using the legend, answer the following questions:
    • Approximately how many days of snow cover does the northern part of the state experience?
    • How many days of snow cover are there in the southern half of the state?

15. Before we search a different part of the world, let's add this site to our list of Favorites or Bookmarks so we can access it later.
16. Click the **ROAD MAP** tab again.
17. In the search box under the ROAD MAP tab, type **Ellis Island** and click **FIND A PLACE**.
18. Click the **SATELLITE** tab at the top. Zoom in and out and move around to see the location of the Statue of Liberty.

MAP TO YOUR HOME

1. Open your browser if it is not already open.
2. Type the following into the Address box: **www. mapquest.com** and press **Enter**; press **return** if you are using a Mac.

The following site should open:

Figure 3-05   The MapQuest Web site

3. Click **Maps** at the top of the screen.
4. Type the street address of your school in the Address or Intersection box. You also need to type the city and state or the zip code in the appropriate boxes. You may need to ask your teacher if you don't know the address.
5. Click **Search**.

You should see a map of your school. Hopefully, you will recognize some of the street names. There are zoom icons at the left side of this screen as well. Feel free to zoom in closer or to zoom out.

Now let's find directions to your home.

6. Scroll back to the top of the site. Under the address of your school, you will see links that say Directions To and Directions From.
7. Click **Directions From**.

The starting location has been filled in with your school's address. All you need to do is fill in your home address as the Ending Location.

8. Type your street address into the Address or Intersection box.
9. Type your city and state or your zip code in the text boxes.

HINT
Make sure that you spell everything correctly when typing in your address.

10. Click **Get Directions**. Scroll down to see the directions.
11. Share your map with a friend in class.
12. Add this site to your list of Favorites or Bookmarks.

NOW YOU TRY IT!
Open the Web site **www.nationalgeographic.com/ mapmachine**. Search for your school's address. View the satellite map and zoom in to see if you can find your school.

Lesson 3-3 HOMEWORK HELP

IN THIS LESSON, WE WILL:
> View homework help sites
> Play games related to class work
> Translate words online

In this lesson, you will learn how to use an online homework help site to assist you when you are working away from school. These sites will also help you study and remember the information you learn in school. Most homework help sites allow you to practice the concepts you learned in school, play games to reinforce your knowledge, and ask an expert for help.

HOMEWORK HELP

1. Open your browser if it is not already open.
2. Type the following into the Address box: **www.factmonster.com** and press **Enter**; press **return** if you are using a Mac.

The following screen appears:

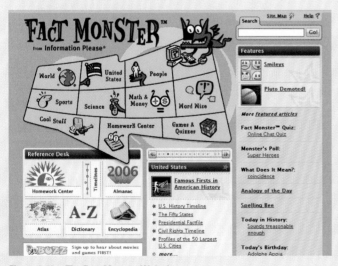

Figure 3-06   The Fact Monster Web site

3. Click the **Homework Center** link.
4. Scroll down to the **Tools for School** section. Under **Science**, click **Conversion Calculator**.
5. Click **common units**. We will now convert a mile into inches. In the **Convert from:** box select mile. In the **Convert to:** box select inch. Press the **convert!** button for your answer.
6. Let's bookmark this site for later. Do you remember how to add it to your list of Favorites or Bookmarks?

MORE HOMEWORK HELP

1. Open your browser if it is not already open.
2. Type the following into the Address box: **http://school.discovery.com/homeworkhelp/ bjpinchbeck** and press **Enter**; press **return** if you are using a Mac.

The following screen appears:

Figure 3-07   The BJ Pinchbeck Homework Helper site

3. Click the **Foreign Languages** link in the middle of the screen.

4. Scroll down and click a translator site.

5. Translate the word "school" into the following four languages: Spanish, Italian, French, and German.

6. Write down your answers on a sheet of paper.

7. Check out some of the links for other subjects.

8. Add this site to your list of Favorites or Bookmarks.

NOW YOU TRY IT!

Go back to the BJ Pinchbeck Homework Helper site. Click the Science link. Scroll through the links and explore the sites listed.

Chapter 3
WRAP UP

> On many Web sites, you can just press Enter (**return** if you are using a Mac) after typing the text in a search box.

> Many dictionary sites also offer synonyms and antonyms.

> A synonym is a word that means the same as another word.

> An antonym is a word that means the opposite of another word.

> Some encyclopedia sites require a subscription in order for you access the articles.

> Free, open content encyclopedias are created and edited by the Web site's viewers.

> Any Web site that is created and edited by its viewers is called a wiki.

> When you want to search for information using exactly the words that you entered in that order, place the words inside quotation marks.

> Online maps can usually be zoomed in closer.

> A satellite map is an aerial photograph taken from a satellite in the Earth's atmosphere.

> Some online maps also give driving directions from one place to another.

> On homework help sites, visitors can play games, practice concepts learned in class, or contact an expert for additional help.

WHAT DO YOU KNOW?

1. On many Web sites, you can just press _____ after typing text in a search box.
    - A. Enter
    - B. Shift
    - C. Space
    - D. Ctrl

2. A word that means the same as another word is called a(n) _____.
    - A. euphemism
    - B. antonym
    - C. singular
    - D. synonym

3. A word that means the opposite of another word is called a(n) _____.
   A. euphemism
   B. antonym
   C. singular
   D. synonym

4. Some encyclopedia sites require a subscription to access the articles.
   A. true
   B. false

5. A Web site where all content is created and edited by its viewers is called a _____.
   A. weirdo
   B. wiki
   C. willi
   D. wylie

6. If you want to search for articles containing the exact string of words in the specific order that you entered them, you can place _____ around the words.
   A. asterisks
   B. hyphens
   C. quotation marks
   D. exclamation marks

7. When searching, you should be sure to place a space before and after the quotation marks in the search box.
   A. true
   B. false

PROJECT PRACTICE

Enter the hallway of the Word Central Web site. Go to the second floor and enter the Computer Lab. Type the sentence "The quick brown fox jumped over the lazy dog" into the text box. Use the "Secret Cipher" and encode the message.

Open BJ Pinchbeck's homework help site. Click Math. Open the "Ask Dr. Math" link. Click Middle School and then Puzzles. Scroll down and see if you can answer the "1 Dollar, 50 Coins" problem.

Open the Web site **www.factmonster.com**. Click People, then click Women of Influence. Click Women Nobel Prize Winners. Read through the list. Who was the first woman to win a Nobel Prize? What for?

You are trying to do your science homework. However, you are not exactly sure of the word you should use. Using the Hyperdictionary Web site, find the definitions of the following two words: beaker and beacon. Which one is the word you want to use when discussing your science experiment?

8. A map that is a series of photographs taken from a satellite in the Earth's atmosphere is called a _____ map.
   A. theme
   B. physical
   C. road
   D. satellite

9. The _____ is a chart that illustrates the symbols or colors on a map.
   A. definition
   B. legend
   C. paper
   D. script

10. Which of the following is not something you can do on most homework help sites?
   A. Ask an expert for help.
   B. Play games to reinforce your knowledge.
   C. Practice the concepts you learned in school.
   D. All of the above are activities that can be done.

BUDDY PROJECT

Using your weekly spelling list, work with a partner to find a synonym and an antonym for each word on the list. Use the Hyperdictionary Web site.

GUIDED PRACTICE

Open the Web site **www.infoplease.com/thesaurus**. On the right-hand side, click the link that says "Frequently Misspelled Words." Choose approximately ten words from the list. Sit down with your parent or guardian and take turns quizzing each other on the spelling of the words on the list.

Chapter 4

SEARCHING AND RETRIEVING

Have you ever seen the painting of the Mona Lisa? What about the famous ceiling in the Sistine Chapel? Before the Internet and the World Wide Web, these great works of art, along with countless others by famous painters such as Rembrandt, Picasso, or Monet, could only be fully appreciated by visiting museums. Today, it is possible to view them using an online image database. Reproductions of these masterpieces can even be ordered so that you can hang them in your own home.

IN THIS CHAPTER, WE WILL:

> Use a search engine to find information about a specific topic
> Click through the links of a directory to find information
> Explore other features of a search engine
> Refine a search
> Use the printer-friendly option to print a recipe
> Copy text from the Internet

> Paste text into a word processor
> Search for a photo using an image database
> Copy a photo from the Internet
> Paste a photo into a word processor
> Save a photo from the Internet
> Learn the difference between MLA and APA style
> Create a citation using an online citation maker
> Format text with a hanging indent

Lesson 4-1
SEARCH ENGINES AND DIRECTORIES

IN THIS LESSON, WE WILL:
> Use a search engine to find information about a specific topic
> Click through the links of a directory to find information
> Explore other features of a search engine
> Refine a search
> Use the printer-friendly option to print a recipe

KEY TERMS
directory
search engine

In this lesson, you will learn how to search the Internet using a search engine and a directory to discover more information about specific topics. We will also learn how to narrow or refine our search.

HINT
Remember if you are using Safari as your browser on a Macintosh, your screen might look slightly different.

SEARCH ENGINES

1. Open your browser.
2. Type the following into the Address box: **www.yahooligans.com** and press **Enter**; press **return** if you are using a Mac.

The following screen appears:

Reproduced with permission of Yahoo! Inc. © 2005 by Yahoo! Inc. YAHOO! and the YAHOO! logo are trademarks of Yahoo! Inc.

Figure 4-01   The Yahooligans Web site

Yahooligans is a **search engine**, which means that it will search the Internet for Web sites that contain specific key words that you enter. Yahooligans is also very similar to Google or Yahoo, but the content is kid-friendly.

3. We want to find out more about monkeys. Type the word **monkey** in the search box and press **Enter**; press **return** if you are using a Mac. How many Web site matches did you find?
4. Click one of the links about spider monkeys. Can you find out how big a spider monkey grows?

IMPORTANT VOCABULARY TERMS

search engine: a Web site that searches the Internet for other sites that contain specific key word(s) that are entered in the text box.

DIRECTORY

1. We need to go back to the main Yahooligans Web site. You can either click the Back button until you reach it or, if you are still on the Yahooligans Web site, you can click the Yahooligans logo in the top left part of your screen to link you back to the main Web page.

Now, let's search for information about monkeys using the categories on the screen. When a Web site has categories to narrow the search process, that is called a **directory**.

2. Click the **Science & Nature** link.

Now you see many links related only to science and nature; these are all more categories. Notice that some of the categories have a number in parentheses, and some of them are followed by the @ symbol. The number refers to how many Web sites were found about that topic. The @ symbol means that you can narrow the category even further.

3. Click the **Animals** category.
4. Next, click the **Mammals** category.
5. Mammals is a pretty broad category. Let's get more specific by clicking **Primates**.
6. You should now find a link specific to **Spider Monkeys**. How many Web sites were found?

Using a directory gives similar results to using a search engine. If you know exactly what you are looking for, it is probably easier to use a search engine. However, if you are not sure, or if you want broader information, a directory is the way to go.

Yahooligans also has many other fun features along the left side of the screen such as: TV, Music, Games, Science, Horoscopes, and lots more. Take some time to explore these links. Try asking "Earl" a question that has kept you puzzled or sending a friend an E-card.

7. You have probably realized that this is a very fun site, and it would be helpful to you in the future. Add it to your list of Favorites or Bookmarks.

directory: a Web site that has categories that narrow the subject of a search.

MORE SEARCH ENGINES

The next search engine we will explore is KidsClick!

1. Type the following into the Address box: **www. kidsclick.org** and press **Enter**; press **return** if you are using a Mac.

The following screen appears:

Figure 4-02   The KidsClick! Web site

This Web site is also a search engine with a directory of categories. The great thing about this site is that all of the sites that it finds have been evaluated for content by librarians across the country, so we know it provides safe and accurate information.

We are going to search for the word "monkey" again to see what kind of results this search engine retrieves.

2. Type the word **monkey** in the Search box. Press **Enter**; press **return** if you are using a Mac, or click **Search**.

How many results did you find this time? Are they the same results as your previous search?

3. Use the Back arrow to get back to the main KidsClick! page.

4. This time, use the directory to find information about monkeys. First click **Science & Math**, then click **Animals**, and next click **Mammals (General)**. Look through the list of sites to find some about monkeys.

Let's try one more common search engine.

5. Type the following into the Address box: **www. askforkids.com** and press **Enter**; press **return** if you are using a Mac.

The following screen appears:

Figure 4-03   The Ask for Kids Web site

The Ask for Kids site opens up.

6. Type **spider monkey** in the text box and click **Search**.

7. You should find one site about the Brown-Headed Spider Monkey. Click this link. Does it give you similar information to the previous two search engines?

8. Click the Back button. You will also see a drop-down arrow displaying other matches to provide information about the Central American Spider Monkey, the Black Spider Monkey, and the White-Bellied Spider Monkey. Choose one of the other spider monkeys and click **Go**. Are they all about the same size?

9. Click the **Back** arrow twice to return to the main Ask for Kids site.

10. Try out some of the study tools by clicking some of the books on the right.

11. Add this site to your list of Favorites or Bookmarks.

REFINING YOUR SEARCH

Sometimes when you are searching for a topic, you get so many results that you are not able (nor do you have the time) to look at all of them. Next, let's learn about refining our search so we get only the information that we really want.

1. Type the following into the Address box: **www.google.com** and press **Enter**; press **return** on the Mac.

The following screen appears:

Figure 4-04   The Google Web Site

You are interested in making cookies for your mom's birthday.

2. Type **cookies** in the search box. Press **Enter**; press **return** if you are using a Mac.

Your search results probably total in the millions. Let's refine our search a little.

3. Change the search to be **chocolate chip cookies** and press **Enter**; press **return** on the Mac.

That reduced the number of results somewhat. However, let's be sure that we are getting only "chocolate chip" cookies and not chocolate/peanut butter cookies or even butterscotch chip cookies.

4. Put quotations around the words **"chocolate chip"** in your search box (leave the word **cookies** outside of the quotations). Press **Enter**; press **return** if you are using a Mac.

We still get too many results. Let's refine the search some more. We remembered that mom is allergic to oatmeal. Let's change our search to take out cookies made with oatmeal.

5. Add **-oatmeal** at the end of the text in the search box and press **Enter**; press **return** on the Mac.

TIPS & TRICKS

Adding a minus sign before a word when searching will make sure that any Web sites containing that word are not included in the results. There should not be any spaces between the minus sign and the word.

Now how many results do you have? Let's refine the search again. Mom loves walnuts. Let's be sure that we are searching for walnuts too.

6. Add **+walnuts** in the search box. Press **Enter**; press **return** if you are using a Mac.

TIPS & TRICKS

To be sure that your search results include a specific word, add a plus sign before the word in the search text box. Again, there should not be any spaces between the plus sign and the word.

The number of results is now much smaller than our original search. However, let's refine the search once more. Remember we are making cookies, so we want to be sure that our results include a recipe!

7. Add **+recipe** to the end of the text in the search box. The search box should now read: **"chocolate chip" cookies -oatmeal +walnuts +recipe**. Press **Enter**; press **return** if you are using a Mac.

Now we can feel pretty confident that every site we click will give us a recipe for chocolate chip cookies with walnuts and without oatmeal.

8. Look through the recipes and select one that sounds good.

9. Most recipe sites will have an option to print just the recipe. It may say *Print Recipe, Print 3×5 or 4×6 card*, or even *Printer-friendly version*. Choose one of these options and print the recipe.

NOW YOU TRY IT!

Open the Web site **www.yahooligans.com.** Search for Earth Day. Skim through the search results to find out who helped make Earth Day an international holiday. What year did Earth Day actually become an official, international holiday?

Lesson 4-2 RETRIEVING INFORMATION

IN THIS LESSON, WE WILL:
> Copy text from the Internet
> Paste text into a word processor
> Search for a photo using an image database
> Copy a photo from the Internet
> Paste a photo into a word processor
> Save a photo from the Internet

KEY TERMS
Image toolbar
pixel
thumbnail

In this lesson, you will learn how to retrieve information such as text and photos from the Internet.

RETRIEVING TEXT

Let's say that you are doing a research project on the pyramids of ancient Egypt.

1. Type the following into the Address box: **www. nationalgeographic.com/pyramids**. Press **Enter**; press **return** if you are using a Mac.

The following screen appears:

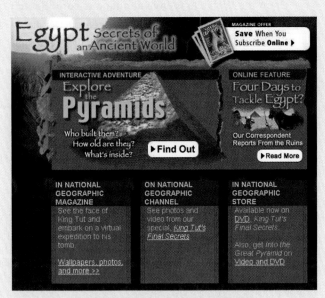

Figure 4-05   The National Geographic Pyramids Web site

HINT
Remember, your screen may look slightly different if you are using a Mac.

2. Click the **Find Out** button in the middle of the screen.

This looks like a perfect bit of information for the report. We have decided to use a sentence directly from the Web site. Instead of rewriting the sentence, we can just copy and paste it into our word processing program.

Anytime you use text or photos from the Internet or a book, you need to give credit to the author. Don't worry, you'll learn how to do that in the next lesson.

3. Scroll down to the section entitled "Who Built the Pyramids?"
4. Use your mouse to select the sentence "An estimated 20,000 to 30,000 workers built the Pyramids at Giza over 80 years." at the beginning of the fifth paragraph in that section.

IMPORTANT VOCABULARY TERMS

thumbnail: a small version of a photo.

5. To copy the sentence, you can **right-click** your mouse and choose **Copy** or you can hold down **Ctrl** and press the letter **C**. On the Mac, press **Ctrl + click** and select **Copy** or press **Command + C**.

TIPS & TRICKS

You can also click Edit from the menu bar and choose Copy to copy text.

6. Open your word processing program and paste the text. In order to paste text, you can right-click and choose **Paste** or hold down **Ctrl** and press the letter **V**. On the Mac, press **Ctrl + click** and select **Paste** or press **Command + V**.
7. That's it! Now all you need to do is add quotation marks on either side of the sentence to show that we will be copying it word for word.

TIPS & TRICKS

You can also click Edit from the menu bar and choose Paste to paste the text.

RETRIEVING PHOTOS

Sometimes you want to find a photo for a school assignment. You could first try to use the graphics option in your word processing program. However, you may not find exactly what you are looking for here, especially if you need a picture of a specific person or place.

1. Open your browser and type the following into the Address box: **www.google.com**. Press **Enter**; press **return** if you are using a Mac.
2. Since we are looking for photos, click **Images** at the top of the screen.
3. Type **Giza pyramids** in the search box and press **Enter**; press **return** if you are using a Mac.

You will see many pages of pyramid photos. These small photos are called **thumbnails**.

4. Find a photo that includes several of the Giza pyramids.

HINT

You can click Next at the bottom of the Web page to see more photos.

Lesson 4-2 RETRIEVING INFORMATION

IMPORTANT VOCABULARY TERMS

pixel: a single point on a photo; the word is created from the words "picture" and "element."

Image toolbar: a small toolbar that appears in the upper left corner of a photo with buttons for saving, printing, e-mailing, and opening the pictures folder.

All photos contain information about the photo below it. The number of pixels, the file size, and the file type are listed. A **pixel** is a single point on a photo. The word pixel is made from "picture" and "element." When looking for a good-quality photo, more pixels and a bigger file size equal a clearer image. The Web site where the photo is stored is also listed.

5. Click the thumbnail photo to be transferred to the site containing the actual photo.

6. Next, click the thumbnail photo at the top of the page or click the link at the top of the screen that says "See full-size image."

The full-size image appears on the page. You have two options to get the photo to your word processing program: copy and paste, or save the photo and then insert it in the word processing program. We will cover both ways.

7. To copy the photo, place your mouse pointer over the photo and right-click. Then click **Copy**. On the Mac, press **Ctrl + click** and select **Copy Image**.

8. Minimize the browser and open your word processing program. Paste the photo—do you remember the ways to paste that we discussed earlier in this lesson?

9. Minimize your word processing program and maximize the browser so we can see the selection of pyramid photos again.

Now, instead of copying the photo, let's save it. In Internet Explorer, when you place your mouse pointer on the photo, you should see a small toolbar in the upper left corner of the photo. This toolbar is called the **Image toolbar** and contains buttons for saving, printing, e-mailing, and opening the pictures folder.

Figure 4-06   The Image toolbar

10. Click the picture of the disk on the Image toolbar to save the photo. Save the photo to your folder on the network.

11. Open your word processing program and insert the photo from your disk.

Photos are placed differently in all word processing programs. Be sure to ask your teacher if you don't know how to insert it.

NOW YOU TRY IT!

Using Google's Image search, search for Olympics. Find the Olympic logo that will be used in the 2012 Olympics in London. Copy and paste it into your word processing program.

Lesson 4-3 CITING YOUR SOURCES

IN THIS LESSON, WE WILL:
> Learn the difference between MLA and APA style
> Create a citation using an online citation maker
> Format text with a hanging indent

KEY TERMS
hanging indent
plagiarism

We know that we can find lots of great things on the Internet. However, when we use the information we find on the Internet, even if we paraphrase it, it is important to give credit to the person(s) who wrote it. If we don't, that is **plagiarism**, and it is not only unethical, but illegal.

ONLINE CITATION CREATOR

Although most people know that they need to credit an author when using his or her text or ideas, they might not know how to write or format the citation. We can find help writing citations by using the Internet.

1. Open your browser, if it is not already open.
2. Type the following into the Address box: **www. citationmachine.net** and press **Enter**; press **return** if you are using a Mac.

The following screen appears:

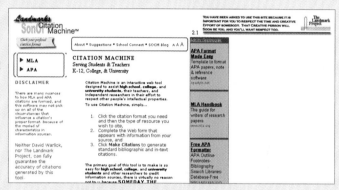

Figure 4-07   The Citation Machine Web site

This site is great because it will help you create a citation for a variety of materials like books, magazines, encyclopedias, and even the Internet!

The first thing we need to decide when creating a citation is the style that's necessary. There are two major styles of writing a citation: APA (American Psychological Association) style and MLA (Modern Language Association) style. For our purposes, we will use MLA style to create our citation because that is the style most commonly used in middle schools and high schools. APA style is used most often in colleges and universities.

IMPORTANT VOCABULARY TERMS

plagiarism: the act of copying text or ideas from another person and claiming them as your own.

Lesson 4-3 CITING YOUR SOURCES

IMPORTANT VOCABULARY TERMS

hanging indent: text formatted so that the first line "hangs over" the remaining indented lines.

3. Click **MLA** on the left side.

Let's give credit for the sentence that we copied from the National Geographic Web site in the last lesson.

4. Under NON-PRINT, click **Web Page**.

All we need to do is fill in the text boxes with the correct information, and the site will create the citation for us. Let's get started!

5. You can skip the first two text boxes since the site did not have an author.

If you are viewing a Web page with an article, you will often see an author listed near the text or title of the article. The author is also sometimes listed at the bottom of the page near the copyright date.

6. Next to "Title of the Web Page," type **Explore the Pyramids**.
7. Next to "Title of the web site," type **Egypt: Secrets of an Ancient World**.
8. Next to "Publishing or last revision date," type **2006**.

9. The "Organization" is **National Geographic Society**.
10. The "Date accessed" is today's date in the following format: **DD MMM YYYY**. It should be filled in for you.
11. The "URL" is **http://www.nationalgeographic.com/pyramids/pyramids.html**.

The last text box is only used when quoting the article and listing the source within the text of a research paper. Since we are creating citations to be written on a single sheet like a bibliography, we are going to leave the last box empty.

12. Click **Submit**.

Your citation appears on the page. You can either handwrite the citation on a piece of paper or copy and paste it into your word processing program.

Be sure to format the text as shown on the screen with a **hanging indent**, wherein the first line "hangs over" the remaining indented lines.

IMPORTANT INFORMATION

In Microsoft Word, select the text. Click Format, and then Paragraph. Under Special, choose Hanging by 0.5" to create a hanging indent.

MORE ONLINE CITATION MAKERS

We are going to do one more citation. This citation will be for the photo that we copied from the Google Web site.

1. Type the following into the Address box: **www. noodletools.com** and press **Enter**; press **return** if you are using a Mac.

The following screen appears:

Figure 4-08   The NoodleTools Web site

NoodleBib has two options available: a subscription service and free usage. If your school has subscribed to this site, you have the capability to create an entire bibliography with several citations and export it to your word processor. However, since we only need to create one citation, the free tools will work fine.

2. Under the blue bar that says "Free Tools," click **NoodleBib Express**.
3. At the next screen, click **MLA**.
4. At the top of the screen, click the arrow to open the pull-down menu. Scroll down until you find **Painting, Sculpture, or Photograph**.
5. Click **Go**.
6. Scroll to the bottom of the page, if necessary, and click **Next**.
7. Choose the **Online** option button and click **Next**.
8. Click the corresponding option button to select the following choices:
   - A documentary photograph
   - Free
   - Path
9. Click **Next**.
10. Scroll down, if necessary, and type **Giza pyramids** next to "Title of image (or description of subject)."

11. Scroll down a little further and type **www. google.com** under "Unique URL where path starts."

12. In the next text box, "Path," type **Giza pyramids**.

13. Scroll all the way to the bottom and click **Generate Citation**.

That's it! Your citation should look like the following (of course, the date will be different):

Giza pyramids. Photograph. 13 July 2006 <http://www.google.com>. Path: Giza pyramids.

Again, you can either handwrite the citation or copy and paste it into your word processing program.

NOW YOU TRY IT!

Using the Citation Machine, create an MLA citation for a book. The title of the book is *The Great Brain Reforms*. The author is John D. Fitzgerald. It was published by Bantam Doubleday Dell Publishing Group, Inc. in New York in 1973.

Chapter 4
WRAP UP

> A search engine searches the Internet for Web sites that contain specific key words.

> A directory is a Web site that has categories that narrow the subject of a search.

> Some search engines also have directories for additional searching possibilities.

> To search a specific string of text, place quotation marks around the words.

> To include a specific word in a search, place a plus sign before the word.

> To exclude a specific word from a search, place a minus sign before the word.

> Hold Ctrl and press the letter C or right-click and choose Copy to copy text. On the Mac, hold the Command key and press C or Ctrl + click and choose Copy to copy text.

> Hold Ctrl and press the letter V or right-click and choose Paste to paste text. On the Mac, hold the Command key and press V or Ctrl + click and choose Paste to paste text.

> Photos can be copied or saved from online image databases.

> A thumbnail is a smaller version of a photograph.

> The more pixels a photo has, the clearer the image.

> If you copy text or ideas from the Internet or anywhere else, you need to give credit to the author.

> MLA style is most commonly used in middle and high schools to create citations.

> A hanging indent is where all lines are indented except the first line.

WHAT DO YOU KNOW?

1. A _____ is a Web site that searches the Internet for other sites that contain specific key word(s) that are entered in a text box.
   A. search engine
   B. directory
   C. search box
   D. database

2. All search engines also contain directories.
   A. true
   B. false

3. To search for a specific string of text, place an asterisk on either side of the words.
   A. true
   B. false

4. To exclude a specific word from a search, type a _____ before the word.
   A. plus sign
   B. question mark
   C. minus sign
   D. asterisk

5. To include a specific word in a search, type a _____ before the word.
   A. plus sign
   B. question mark
   C. minus sign
   D. asterisk

6. There should not be any spaces between the plus sign and the word you want included when searching.
   A. true
   B. false

7. The keyboard shortcut to copy is _____.
   A. Ctrl + P
   B. Ctrl + C
   C. Ctrl + V
   D. Ctrl + S

PROJECT PRACTICE

You have been given the assignment to write a haiku poem about the weather. Open the Web site, **www.askforkids.com**. Search for haiku to refresh your memory as to the rules of a haiku. Write a poem about weather.

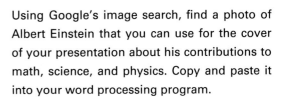

Using Google's image search, find a photo of Albert Einstein that you can use for the cover of your presentation about his contributions to math, science, and physics. Copy and paste it into your word processing program.

Open the Web site **www.yahooligans.com**. Using the directory, search for holidays. Find Cinco de Mayo and answer the following questions: When is it celebrated? Why is it important? How was it started?

Open the Web site **www.yahooligans.com**. Search for the Loch Ness Monster. Using the sites found, search for the answers to the following questions:
- What is the name of the lake where the Loch Ness Monster, or Nessie, is claimed to live?
- When was the first photo of the Loch Ness Monster taken?
- How big is the Loch Ness Monster estimated to be?

8. A small version of the original photo is called a _____.
   A. thumbnail
   B. pixel
   C. fingernail
   D. pixie

9. The word pixel is made from the words "picture" and "element."
   A. true
   B. false

10. The act of copying text or ideas from another person and claiming them as your own is called _____.
    A. cheating
    B. copying
    C. plagiarism
    D. citations

11. The most common style for creating a citation in middle school and high school is _____.
    A. MLA
    B. AOA
    C. MIA
    D. APA

BUDDY PROJECT

Your class is considering getting a pet. Work with a partner to research an appropriate animal on **www. yahooligans.com.** Find a photo of the animal on Google's image search. Write some reasons why your choice would be great for a class pet and paste the photo into your word processing program.

GUIDED PRACTICE

Your family has decided to go on a vacation to Italy. Using the Yahooligans or Ask for Kids search engines, find out some of the great things you can do while on vacation. Make a list of the major attractions you want to see while there.

Glossary

A

Address Book: file on your computer that holds names and e-mail addresses.

antonym: a word that means the opposite of another word.

Attach button: click this to send a file or document along with your e-mail message.

B

Bcc: text box: an e-mail address is typed in this box to send a copy of a message; however, the receiver does not know it has been sent to someone else.

blog: online personal journal; short for Web log.

browser: a software program, such as Internet Explorer, Netscape Navigator, or Safari, that allows you to connect to the Internet.

C

Cc: text box: an e-mail address is typed in this box to send a copy of the message; the receiver knows it has been sent to the other person.

chat room: virtual room where many people can communicate with each other.

cyberbullying: sending rude e-mails, gossiping, or spreading rumors about another person online.

D

directory: a Web site that has categories that narrows the subject of a search.

domain extension: the last part of the URL indicating the type of Web site.

E

E-card: greeting card that is opened in a person's e-mail box.

e-mail: electronic mail.

emoticons: also known as smileys; expressions you create from the characters on your keyboard to add humor and personality to the message.

F

Favorites: Web sites that are saved into a special folder on the computer for easy retrieval. When using a Mac, these are called Bookmarks.

flaming: sending angry e-mail messages.

H

hanging indent: text formatted so that the first line "hangs over" the remaining indented lines.

home page: the Web page that appears when the browser is opened.

HTML: stands for HyperText Markup Language.

Glossary

hyperlink: a picture, object, or different colored text that will take you to another part of a Web site, a different Web site, or a file for more information.

I

Image toolbar: a small toolbar that appears in the upper left corner of a photo with buttons for saving, printing, e-mailing, and opening the pictures folder.

Internet Service Provider (ISP): a company that provides the connection service to the Internet. The ISP is the middleman between your computer and the Internet.

Internet: a very large network that connects millions of computers around the world.

L

legend: chart that illustrates the symbols or colors on a map.

M

menu bar: the row of words across the top of the screen that "pull down" to reveal other commands.

modem: a piece of equipment that lets computers "talk" to other computers using telephone lines, cable lines, or a wireless connection. It can be internal or external.

N

netiquette: guidelines for polite online interaction; the word is formed from Internet and etiquette.

P

pixel: a single point on a photo; the word is created from the words "picture" and "element."

plagiarism: the act of copying text or ideas from another person and claiming them as your own.

S

satellite map: aerial photographs taken from a satellite in the Earth's atmosphere.

scroll bars: the sliding bars found along the right and bottom of the screen, which allow you to see other parts of a long or wide Web page.

search engine: a Web site that searches the Internet for other sites that contain specific key word(s) that are entered in the text box.

Send button: click this to send the message.

Standard Buttons toolbar: contains shortcuts for many common tools such as back, forward, refresh, stop, and home.

Subject: textbox: tells what the message is about. The receiver can see the subject of the message before opening it.

surfing the Web: slang for searching the World Wide Web.

synonym: a word that means the same as another word.

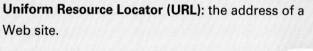
T

thumbnail: a small version of a photo.

title bar: the blue bar that runs across the top of the screen that tells the name of the Web site as well as the name of the browser.

To: text box: where you type the e-mail address of the person you want to send a message to.

U

Uniform Resource Locator (URL): the address of a Web site.

W

wiki: a Web site where all content is created and edited by its viewers.

World Wide Web: a system of Internet servers that support HTML documents, allowing users to follow links to other pages, documents, or graphics.

Index

Index

Photo Credits

Chapter 1:

Chapter Opening photo	A family prepares dinner using recipes they found while searching the Web.	© Ronnie Kaufman/Getty Images
Figure 1-01	www.dce.k12.wi.us/midschool	D.C. Everest Middle School, Weston, WI
Figure 1-05	www.pbskids.org	The screen capture taken from pbs.org contains copyrighted material of the Public Broadcasting Service.
Figure 1-06	www.pbskids.org/cyberchase	The screen capture taken from pbs.org contains copyrighted material of the Public Broadcasting Service.

Chapter 2:

Chapter Opening photo	The e-mail button on a computer screen.	© Crowther & Carter/Getty Images
Figure 2-02	www.pbskids.org/license	The screen capture taken from pbs.org contains copyrighted material of the Public Broadcasting Service.
Figure 2-04	www.hallmark.com	Courtesy of Hallmark Cards, Inc.

Chapter 3:

Chapter Opening photo	A teenager plays video games on his computer.	© Janine Wiedel Photolibrary/Alamy
Figure 3-02	www.wordcentral.com	By permission. From Merriam-Webster's Word Central (www.WordCentral.com) ©2006 by Merriam-Webster, Incorporated (www.Merriam-Webster.com).
Figure 3-03	www.infoplease.com/encyclopedia	©www.infoplease.com
Figure 3-04	www.nationalgeographic.com/mapmachine	Courtesy, Nationalgeographic.com
Figure 3-05	www.mapquest.com	The MapQuest.com logo is a registered trademark of MapQuest, Inc. MapQuest.com content ©2006 MapQuest, Inc. Used with permission.
Figure 3-06	www.factmonster.com	Courtesy, FactMonster.com
Figure 3-07	school.discovery.com/homeworkhelp/bjpinchbeck	Courtesy, Discovery Education

Chapter 4:

Chapter Opening photo	Visitors to a museum view some famous works of art.	© Graeme Harris/Getty Images
Figure 4-01	www.yahooligans.com	Reproduced with permission of Yahoo! Inc. ©2005 by Yahoo! Inc. YAHOO and the YAHOO! logo are trademarks of Yahoo! Inc.
Figure 4-02	www.kidsclick.org	Courtesy, KidsClick.org
Figure 4-03	www.askforkids.com	©2006 AskForKids.com—All Rights Reserved.
Figure 4-04	www.google.com	Courtesy, Google.com
Figure 4-05	www.nationalgeographic.com/pyramids	Courtesy, Nationalgeographic.com
Figure 4-07	www.citationmachine.net	Citation Machine™ is a free service provided by David Warlick and The Landmark Project.
Figure 4-08	www.noodletools.com	Reprinted by permission © NoodleTools, Inc. http://www.NoodleTools.com